# Orbit 7

## DAVID ORME

Orbit 7
by David Orme
Illustrated by Jorge Mongiovi and Ulises Carpintero
Cover photograph: © Janne Ahvo

Published by Ransom Publishing Ltd.
Radley House, 8 St. Cross Road, Winchester, Hampshire SO23 9HX
**www.ransom.co.uk**

ISBN      978 184167 454 4

First published in 2011

Originally published in 1998 by Stanley Thornes Publishers Ltd.

A CIP catalogue record of this book is available from the British Library.

Printed and bound in India by Nutech Print Services

# CONTENTS

# 1

# A STRANGE MESSAGE

'This is Orbit 7 calling ground control. Orbit 7 calling ground control. This is Jones. I don't know what's going on here, but I need help – fast. I am alone, repeat, alone. The others have just vanished! I know it sounds crazy, but they are not on the space station!

'Stand by, ground control. I can see something. There's something outside the station. Something coming closer and closer. It's them – and they're alive! That's not possible!'

'Calm down, Jones! This is ground control. What can you see? I repeat, what can you see? Over.

'Jones! Come in! What is happening up there? Over.'

The ground control team sat staring at the loudspeaker. Jones's voice had stopped. They heard nothing but the whisper of static.

# 2

# RESCUE MISSION

On the space shuttle Golden Lion, the crew were undoing their take-off belts. Co-pilot Will Moss had been part of many missions into space. He still felt sick to start with. His body needed time to get used to zero gravity.

These days, all the crew took pills to stop them being sick. Being sick in weightless conditions was very nasty – the stuff floated everywhere!

Mission captain Sue Clarke was looking at a screen.

'Fifteen minutes to meeting point. We should have them in visual range in five minutes.'

The third member of the crew was Mike Darwin. He was a doctor. When ground control had heard the message from space station Orbit 7, they knew something was seriously wrong. Perhaps Jones had gone mad and killed the others. Dr Darwin was ready for anything.

Soon, they could see Orbit 7 spinning slowly in front of them. Everything seemed normal.

Sue Clarke called ground control.

'Golden Lion to ground control. Everything looks fine from the outside. Five minutes to docking.'

'Copy, Golden Lion. Take care now.'

The shuttle moved closer and closer to the station. The crew heard a thud as the shuttle locked on. A green light came on over the door.

'Ground control, we are now docked. Opening door now.'

There was a hiss and the door swung open.

'O.K. team,' said the captain. 'Let's go for it.'

# THE EMPTY SPACE STATION

Dr Darwin went first. He carried a stun spray in case of trouble. Guns couldn't be used on the space station. A bullet would go straight through the wall. Air would be sucked into space.

There were nine space stations in orbit around the Earth. They were built like giant steel rings. They were used for science experiments and to pass TV, phone calls and the Internet from one part of the Earth to

another. The stations were designed to spin in space, which made some gravity on them. This made life much better for the space station crew.

The rescue team headed towards the living area. It was empty. There was a meal on the table. It was half-eaten. It looked as if someone had left the table in a hurry.

The team moved on to the sleeping rooms. They were empty too. Where could the crew be?

Will sniffed. 'What's that smell?'

There was a faint, sweet smell in the air. Will had noticed it as soon as they had got into the space station. It was stronger here.

'Right,' said Captain Clarke. 'Let's do this properly. We'll start here, and work right round the station. They must be somewhere! We'll stick together in case Jones is waiting to jump us. Keep alert.'

They worked steadily round the space station. Dr Darwin was still in the lead. Captain Clarke came last. She kept checking behind her.

They checked the laboratories first. They were empty. Will Moss pointed to a work-bench.

'Look! Someone was in the middle of an experiment!'

A glass bottle was lying on the bench. It had been knocked over. A sticky green liquid oozed on to the floor. Dr Darwin sniffed it carefully.

'I don't know what it is, but that's where the smell is coming from.'

He picked up the bottle. There was a label on it:

SAMPLE FROM EUROPA
HANDLE WITH CARE

Europa was a moon of Jupiter. Scientists had found simple living things there. Maybe the green liquid was alive!

Dr Darwin carefully put the stopper back in the bottle.

They carried on. They searched the store-rooms, and the big control room. This was the

most important part of the station. Here was
everything they needed to keep the station
running.

Jones had sent his last message from the
control room. Will checked out the radio.

'It's still switched on!'

They all looked out of the small window. It was pointing away from the Earth. Bright stars were burning in the darkness.

'I wonder what Jones thought he saw through this window,' said Captain Clarke. 'Do you think they all went mad, Doc?'

Dr Darwin didn't reply. Will and the captain turned round.

The doctor had gone.

# WHERE IS THE DOCTOR?

Will Moss and Sue Clarke were both tough characters, but they both felt frightened. What was happening on Orbit 7? How had the doctor disappeared without making a sound? He had been standing just behind them! Could Jones be hiding somewhere on the station? Surely not! They had searched everywhere.

The captain made a decision.

'This time, we'll split up. We'll work round the station in opposite directions. Jones could

have been moving ahead of us all the time. We could go round and round the station, and never catch up with him!'

They both had stun sprays. One squirt of this in the face, and you would be knocked out for hours.

The captain set off, towards the living area. Will turned and went the other way. He passed through the laboratory again. He stopped and looked at the green liquid in the bottle. He wondered what experiments the people on the station had been doing on the Europa sample. He guessed that it was top secret.

Boxes were piled up in the storeroom. It was the only place anyone could hide. Will shifted as many boxes as he could and checked behind them. No one was hiding there.

Soon he reached the living area again. He opened all the cupboards and lockers, but there was nothing unusual in them.

At last he got back to the control room. It was empty.

Will felt scared again – very scared. He could feel his whole body shaking.

He had been right round the station.

The captain had vanished.

# 5
# CALLING EARTH

Will tried to control himself. He took deep breaths. The strange, sweet smell seemed to be getting stronger, even though the doctor had closed the bottle.

He sat down at the radio. He needed help.

'This is Orbit 7 calling ground control. Orbit 7 calling ground control. This is Will Moss. I don't know what's going on here, but I need help fast. I am alone, repeat, alone. The others have vanished! I know it sounds crazy, but they are not on the space station!'

He stopped sending. Something had caught his eye. He looked through the window into space. There was something out there. Something was heading towards the station!

'Stand by, ground control. I can see something. There's something outside the station. Something coming closer and closer ...'

Will started to shake again. This time, he couldn't control it. Outside he saw five figures, the space station crew. The captain. The doctor. They had no space suits and yet they seemed alive. They pressed their faces up against the window. They were laughing at Will, laughing like mad people!

'It's them! And they're alive! That's not possible!'

Back on Earth, the ground control team stared at each other. No voice came from the

loudspeaker. They heard nothing but the
whisper of static.

Inside the laboratory, the bottle had fallen
over again. The strange green liquid dripped
on to the floor once more. The smell was even

stronger now, but there was no one on the
station to smell it.

No human being, that is.

Outside the station, the creatures that
looked like humans were heading to Earth.

NOT FOR THE PUB

TOP SE

ZONE 13 FILE

# ABOUT THE AUTHOR

David Orme is an expert on strange, unexplained events. For his protection (and yours) we cannot show a photograph of him.

David created the Zone 13 files to record the cases he studied. Some of these files really do involve aliens, but many do not. Aliens are not everywhere. Just in most places.

These stories are all taken from the Zone 13 files. They will not be here for long. Read them while you can.

But don't close your eyes when you go to sleep at night. **They** will be watching you.